AT YOUR SERVICE

The crowd moves steadily past his window. He is one of 1,100 ticket office clerks who control the issue of 1,280,000 tickets from automatic machines and ticket racks at 174 stations every day.

At your service; ticket office, by Leo Dowd, 1947

London Underground Desk Diary 2019
© Quarto Publishing plc 2018
Text and illustrations © Tfl 13/4992

 ® © TfL 13/4992

First published in 2018 by Frances Lincoln,
an imprint of The Quarto Group.
www.QuartoKnows.com

Astronomical information © Crown
Copyright. Reproduced by permission of
the Controller of Her Majesty's Stationery
Office and the UK Hydrographic Office
(www.ukho.gov.uk).

Publisher's Note: When a national or
religious holiday occurs this is shown by
the relevant country's abbreviation in
capitals. Other days of interest are included.
Every effort is made to ensure calendarial
data and other information is correct at
the time of going to press but the publisher
cannot accept any liability for any errors
or changes.

A catalogue record for this book is
available from the British Library

ISBN: 978-0-7112-3992-0

Printed in China

9 8 7 6 5 4 3 2 1

 TFL OFFICIAL LICENSED PRODUCT

Moon Phases
- ● New Moon
- ☽ First Quarter
- ○ Full Moon
- ☾ Last Quarter

Cover:
Pocket Underground
map, by London
Electric Railway,
c.1932

Back cover:
Whistle; as issued
by LPTB staff,
1933–1947

FSC
www.fsc.org
MIX
Paper from
responsible sources
FSC® C101537

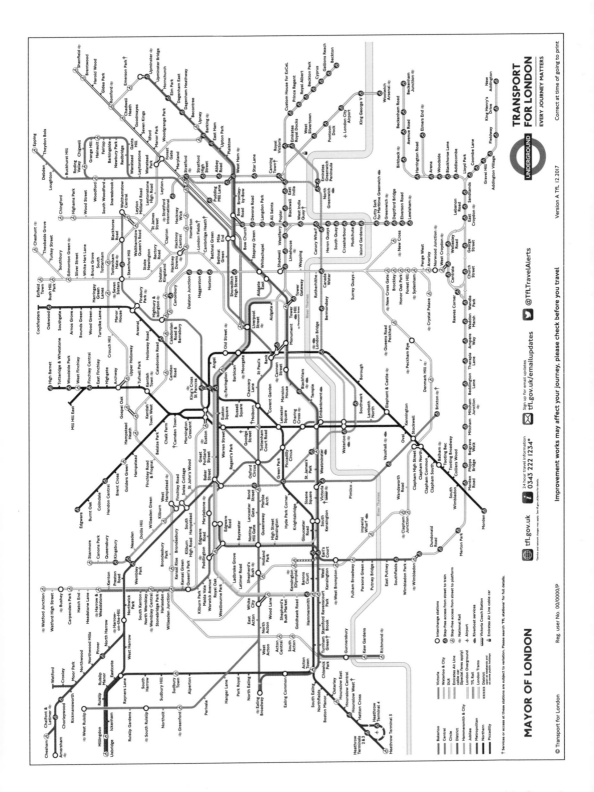

MAYOR OF LONDON

Reg. user No. 00/0000/P

TRANSPORT
FOR LONDON
EVERY JOURNEY MATTERS

UNDERGROUND

Correct at time of going to print

Version A TfL 12.2017

Improvement works may affect your journey, please check before you travel

tfl.gov.uk

24 hour travel information
0343 222 1234*

Sign up for email updates
tfl.gov.uk/emailupdates

@TfLTravelAlerts

© Transport for London

The Tube map is up-to-date at the time of printing, but to view the most recent release please visit tfl.gov.uk

Calendar

2019

January
```
M  T  W  T  F  S  S
      01 02 03 04 05 06
07 08 09 10 11 12 13
14 15 16 17 18 19 20
21 22 23 24 25 26 27
28 29 30 31
```

February
```
M  T  W  T  F  S  S
            01 02 03
04 05 06 07 08 09 10
11 12 13 14 15 16 17
18 19 20 21 22 23 24
25 26 27 28
```

March
```
M  T  W  T  F  S  S
            01 02 03
04 05 06 07 08 09 10
11 12 13 14 15 16 17
18 19 20 21 22 23 24
25 26 27 28 29 30 31
```

April
```
M  T  W  T  F  S  S
01 02 03 04 05 06 07
08 09 10 11 12 13 14
15 16 17 18 19 20 21
22 23 24 25 26 27 28
29 30
```

May
```
M  T  W  T  F  S  S
      01 02 03 04 05
06 07 08 09 10 11 12
13 14 15 16 17 18 19
20 21 22 23 24 25 26
27 28 29 30 31
```

June
```
M  T  W  T  F  S  S
               01 02
03 04 05 06 07 08 09
10 11 12 13 14 15 16
17 18 19 20 21 22 23
24 25 26 27 28 29 30
```

July
```
M  T  W  T  F  S  S
01 02 03 04 05 06 07
08 09 10 11 12 13 14
15 16 17 18 19 20 21
22 23 24 25 26 27 28
29 30 31
```

August
```
M  T  W  T  F  S  S
         01 02 03 04
05 06 07 08 09 10 11
12 13 14 15 16 17 18
19 20 21 22 23 24 25
26 27 28 29 30 31
```

September
```
M  T  W  T  F  S  S
                  01
02 03 04 05 06 07 08
09 10 11 12 13 14 15
16 17 18 19 20 21 22
23 24 25 26 27 28 29
30
```

October
```
M  T  W  T  F  S  S
01 02 03 04 05 06
07 08 09 10 11 12 13
14 15 16 17 18 19 20
21 22 23 24 25 26 27
28 29 30 31
```

November
```
M  T  W  T  F  S  S
            01 02 03
04 05 06 07 08 09 10
11 12 13 14 15 16 17
18 19 20 21 22 23 24
25 26 27 28 29 30
```

December
```
M  T  W  T  F  S  S
                  01
02 03 04 05 06 07 08
09 10 11 12 13 14 15
16 17 18 19 20 21 22
23 24 25 26 27 28 29
30 31
```

2020

January
```
M  T  W  T  F  S  S
      01 02 03 04 05
06 07 08 09 10 11 12
13 14 15 16 17 18 19
20 21 22 23 24 25 26
27 28 29 30 31
```

February
```
M  T  W  T  F  S  S
               01 02
03 04 05 06 07 08 09
10 11 12 13 14 15 16
17 18 19 20 21 22 23
24 25 26 27 28 29
```

March
```
M  T  W  T  F  S  S
                  01
02 03 04 05 06 07 08
09 10 11 12 13 14 15
16 17 18 19 20 21 22
23 24 25 26 27 28 29
30 31
```

April
```
M  T  W  T  F  S  S
         01 02 03 04 05
06 07 08 09 10 11 12
13 14 15 16 17 18 19
20 21 22 23 24 25 26
27 28 29 30
```

May
```
M  T  W  T  F  S  S
            01 02 03
04 05 06 07 08 09 10
11 12 13 14 15 16 17
18 19 20 21 22 23 24
25 26 27 28 29 30 31
```

June
```
M  T  W  T  F  S  S
01 02 03 04 05 06 07
08 09 10 11 12 13 14
15 16 17 18 19 20 21
22 23 24 25 26 27 28
29 30
```

July
```
M  T  W  T  F  S  S
      01 02 03 04 05
06 07 08 09 10 11 12
13 14 15 16 17 18 19
20 21 22 23 24 25 26
27 28 29 30 31
```

August
```
M  T  W  T  F  S  S
               01 02
03 04 05 06 07 08 09
10 11 12 13 14 15 16
17 18 19 20 21 22 23
24 25 26 27 28 29 30
31
```

September
```
M  T  W  T  F  S  S
      01 02 03 04 05 06
07 08 09 10 11 12 13
14 15 16 17 18 19 20
21 22 23 24 25 26 27
28 29 30
```

October
```
M  T  W  T  F  S  S
         01 02 03 04
05 06 07 08 09 10 11
12 13 14 15 16 17 18
19 20 21 22 23 24 25
26 27 28 29 30 31
```

November
```
M  T  W  T  F  S  S
                  01
02 03 04 05 06 07 08
09 10 11 12 13 14 15
16 17 18 19 20 21 22
23 24 25 26 27 28 29
30
```

December
```
M  T  W  T  F  S  S
01 02 03 04 05 06
07 08 09 10 11 12 13
14 15 16 17 18 19 20
21 22 23 24 25 26 27
28 29 30 31
```

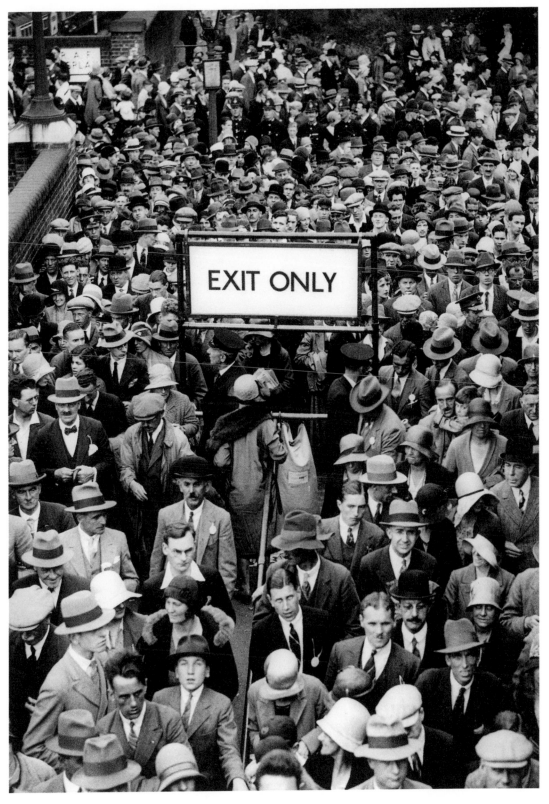

Crowds returning to Colindale station, Topical Press, 28 June 1930

Year planner

January

February

March

Year planner

April

May

June

Year planner

July

August

September

Year planner

October

November

December

Go to Kew, by Maxwell Ashby Armfield, 1915

Important dates

Useful numbers

A stairwell entrance to Tottenham Court Road Underground station, 1907

Transport for London and the London Transport Museum

The modern graphic poster came into use in the 1890s, revolutionizing the fields of publicity, advertising and propaganda.

Transport for London's archives transcend the story of the world's greatest capital city. Celebrating the iconic art and design of the Underground and unique pictures of London, leisure, travel and nature — all life is here.

Transport for London's poster collection covers over 100 years of graphic art and contains some of the best examples of posters as an art form anywhere in the world. The tradition of employing both established and emerging artistic talent to promoting public transport was started by Frank Pick in 1908. Since then, posters have played a key role in the wider vision of corporate transport design. Over 5,000 designs and 800 original artworks are available online. The collection continues to grow and represents a remarkable cross-section of artists displaying a huge range of styles, formats and techniques. There are posters to inform, educate, reassure, entertain and inspire.

The London Transport Museum explores the story of London and its transport system over the last 200 years, highlighting the powerful link between transport and the growth of modern London, culture and society since 1800. The museum cares for over 450,000 items, including the poster collection.

Find out more at www.ltmuseum.co.uk

Jacket issued to London Transport Police, 1934–1958

Explore London

family London

V&A Museum of Childhood, Cambridge Heath Road, London E2 9PA
Closest tube station: Bethnal Green on the Central Line
Find out more at www.vam.ac.uk/moc/
Diana Memorial Playground, Royal Parks, Kensington Gardens, London
Closest tube station: Queensway on the Central Line, Bayswater on the
Circle and District Lines
Find out more at www.royalparks.org.uk/parks/kensington-gardens/things-to-see-and-do/
diana-memorial-playground
London Zoo, Outer Circle Regent's Park, London, NW1 4RY
Closest tube station: Camden Town on the Northern Line, Regent's Park on the Bakerloo Line
Find out more at www.zsl.org/zsl-london-zoo
Coram's Fields, 93 Guilford Street, London WC1N 1DN
Closest tube station: Russell Square on the Piccadilly Line, Kings Cross St Pancras on the
Victoria, Piccadilly, Northern, Hammersmith & City, Circle Lines, Holborn on the Central and
Piccadilly Lines
Find out more at www.coramsfields.org
Science Museum, Exhibition Road, South Kensington, London SW7 2DD
Closest tube station: South Kensington on the District, Circle and Piccadilly Lines
Find out more at www.sciencemuseum.org.uk

free London

The National Gallery, Trafalgar Square, London WC2N 5DN
Closest tube station: Charing Cross on the Northern and Bakerloo Lines, Leicester Square
on the Northern and Piccadilly Lines, Piccadilly Circus on the Piccadilly and Bakerloo Lines,
Embankment on the Northern, Bakerloo, District and Circle Lines
Find out more at www.nationalgallery.org.uk
Choral service at St Paul's Cathedral, St. Paul's Churchyard, London EC4M 8AD
Closest tube station: St Paul's on the Central Line, Mansion House on the District and Circle
Lines, Blackfriars on the District and Circle Lines, Bank on the Central, Northern and Waterloo
& City Lines
Find out more at www.stpauls.co.uk
Richmond Park, Royal Parks, Richmond, London
Closest tube station: Richmond on the District Line
Find out more at www.royalparks.org.uk/parks/richmond-park

quiet London

Postman's Park, St Martin's Le-Grand, London EC1A
Closest tube station: St Paul's on the Central Line
Find out more at www.postmanspark.org.uk
Poetry Library, Level 5 Royal Festival Hall, London SE1 8XX
Closest tube station: Waterloo on the Northern, Bakerloo, Jubilee and Waterloo & City Lines,
Embankment on the District and Circle Lines
Find out more at www.poetrylibrary.org.uk
Southwark Cathedral, London Bridge, London SE1 9DA
Closest tube station: London Bridge on the Northern and Jubilee Lines
Find out more at www.cathedral.southwark.anglican.org

London pubs	**Ye Olde Cheshire Cheese,** 145 Fleet Street, London EC4A 2BU Closest tube station: Blackfriars on the District and Circle Lines, Chancery Lane or St Pauls on the Central Line **The French House,** 49 Dean Street, Soho, London W1D 5BG Closest tube station: Leicester Square on the Northern and Piccadilly Lines, Tottenham Court Road on the Northern and Central Lines, Piccadilly Circus on the Piccadilly and Bakerloo Lines Find out more at www.frenchhousesoho.com **Princess Louise,** 208 High Holborn, London, WC1V 7EP Closest tube station: Holborn on the Central and Piccadilly Lines Find out more at www.princesslouisepub.co.uk **Euston Tap,** 190 Euston Road, London NW1 2EF Closest tube station: Euston on the Northern and Victoria Lines Find out more at www.eustontap.com
shop London	**Golborne Road,** London W10 A hub for thriving North African and Portuguese communities, with plenty of places to eat and drink, vintage fashion and furniture and a regular street market Closest tube station: Westbourne Park or Ladbroke Grove on the Circle and Hammersmith & City Lines **Broadway Market,** London E8 4QJ At the heart of Hackney, a street of independent shops, pubs, restaurants and cafés and a Saturday street market Closest tube station: London Fields on the Overground Find out more at www.broadwaymarket.co.uk **Brixton Village,** Coldharbour Lane, London SW9 8LB A culinary and cultural hub, home to a range of international cafés, restaurants and shops, open late and with live music on a Friday and Saturday Closest tube station: Brixton on the Victoria Line Find out more at www.brixtonmarket.net/brixton-village
London sights	**Tower Bridge,** Tower Bridge Road, London SE1 2UP Closest tube station: Tower Hill on the District and Circle Lines, London Bridge on the Northern and Jubilee Lines Find out more at www.towerbridge.org.uk **Big Ben and the Houses of Parliament,** Westminster, London SW1A 0AA Closest tube station: Westminster on the Circle, District and Jubilee Lines Find out more at www.parliament.uk/visiting **Trafalgar Square,** London WC2N 5DN Closest tube station: Charing Cross on the Northern and Bakerloo Lines **Buckingham Palace,** Westminster, London SW1A 1AA Closest tube station: Victoria on the Circle, District and Victoria Lines, Green Park on the Jubilee, Piccadilly and Victoria Lines, St. James's Park on the Circle and District Lines, Hyde Park Corner on the Piccadilly Line Find out more at www.royal.uk/buckingham-palace

Explore London

London theatreland

The Mousetrap at St Martin's Theatre, West Street, London WC2H 9NZ
Closest tube station: Leicester Square on the Northern and Piccadilly Lines, Tottenham Court Road on the Northern and Central Lines, Charing Cross on the Northern and Bakerloo Lines
Find out more at www.the-mousetrap.co.uk

The Lion King at The Lyceum, 21 Wellington Street, London WC2E 7RQ
Closest tube station: Covent Garden on the Piccadilly Line, Temple on the Circle and District Lines, Embankment on the Northern, Bakerloo, District and Circle Lines
Find out more at www.thelionking.co.uk

Harry Potter and the Cursed Child at Palace Theatre, 113 Shaftesbury Avenue, London WID 5AY
Closest tube station: Tottenham Court Road on the Northern and Central Lines, Leicester Square on the Northern and Piccadilly Lines, Piccadilly Circus on the Piccadilly and Bakerloo Lines
Find out more at www.harrypottertheplay.com/uk

Wicked at Apollo Victoria Theatre, 17 Wilton Road, London SWIV ILG
Closest tube station: Victoria on the Circle, District and Victoria Line
Find out more at www.wickedthemusical.co.uk/london

London nightlife

Soho, London WI
At the heart of the West End, Soho offers a heady mix of dining, drinking and clubbing options, buzzing with activity late into the night with Dean, Frith, Beak and Old Compton streets at the epicentre
Closest tube station: Tottenham Court Road on the Northern and Central Lines, Leicester Square on the Northern and Piccadilly Lines, Piccadilly Circus on the Piccadilly and Bakerloo Lines

Shoreditch, London NI
A cool, creative neighbourhood in east London setting trends with a wide range of dining spots, fashionable clubs and bars surrounding Shoreditch High Street, Great Eastern Street and Old Street
Closest tube station: Old Street on the Northern Line, Shoreditch High Street on the Overground

Covent Garden, London WC2E 7BB
A central, elegant piazza surrounded by award-winning restaurants and theatres
Closest tube station: Covent Garden on the Piccadilly Line
Find out more at www.coventgarden.london

London views

Primrose Hill, London NW3
Closest tube station: Chalk Farm on the Northern Line, St John's Wood on the Jubilee Line
Find out more at www.royalparks.org.uk/parks/the-regents-park/things-to-see-and-do/primrose-hill

The London Eye, Westminster Bridge Road, London SEI 7PB
Closest tube station: Waterloo on the Northern, Bakerloo, Jubilee and Waterloo & City Lines, Embankment on the Northern, Bakerloo, District and Circle Lines, Charing Cross on the Northern and Bakerloo Lines
Find out more at www.londoneye.com

Sky Garden, I Sky Garden Walk, London EC3M 8AF
Closest tube station: Monument on the Circle and District Lines
Find out more at www.skygarden.london

FOR THE Z∞, BOOK TO REGENT'S PARK OR CAMDEN TOWN

For the Zoo book to Regent's Park, by Charles Paine, 1921

HAMPSTEAD

TAKE YOUR SON AND HEIR
WHERE THERE IS SUN AND AIR

WE CARRY DOGS AND FOLDING MAILCARTS.

Hampstead Heath, by Charles Sharland, 1914

Explore London

London culture

British Museum, Great Russell Street, London WC1B 3DG
Closest tube station: Tottenham Court Road on the Northern and Central Lines, Holborn on the Picadilly and Central Lines, Russell Square on the Picadilly Line
Find out more at www.britishmuseum.org
Wellcome Collection, 183 Euston Road, London NW1 2BE
Closest tube station: Euston Square on the Circle, Metropolitan and Hammersmith & City Lines, Euston on the Victoria and Northern Lines, Warren Street on the Victoria and Northern Lines
Find out more at www.wellcomecollection.org
Institute of Contemporary Arts, The Mall, St James's, London SW1Y 5AH
Closest tube station: Charing Cross on the Northern and Bakerloo Lines, Piccadilly Circus on the Piccadilly and Bakerloo Lines
Find out more at www.ica.art

green London

Regent's Park, Chester Road, London NW1
Closest tube station: Regent's Park on the Bakerloo Line, Great Portland Street on the Hammersmith & City, Circle and Metropolitan Lines, Baker Street on the Hammersmith & City, Circle, Jubilee, Metropolitan and Bakerloo Lines, St John's Wood on the Jubilee line, Camden Town on the Northern line
Find out more at www.royalparks.org.uk/parks/the-regents-park
Kew Royal Botanic Gardens, Kew, Richmond TW9 3AE
Closest tube station: Kew Gardens on the Overground and District Lines
Find out more at www.kew.org
Victoria Park, Grove Road, London E3
Closest tube station: Mile End on the Central, Hammersmith & City and District Lines
Find out more at www.towerhamlets.gov.uk/lgnl/leisure_and_culture/parks_and_open_spaces/victoria_park/victoria_park.aspx
Greenwich Park, London SE10
Closest tube station: North Greenwich on the Jubilee Line
Find out more at www.royalparks.org.uk/parks/greenwich-park
Hampstead Heath, London NW3
Closest tube station: Golders Green, Hampstead or Kentish Town on the Northern Line, Hampstead Heath or Gospel Oak on the Overground
Find out more at www.cityoflondon.gov.uk/things-to-do/green-spaces/hampstead-heath/Pages/default.aspx

December & January

31
Monday

New Year's Eve

01
Tuesday

New Year's Day. Holiday, UK, Republic of Ireland, USA, Canada, Australia and New Zealand

02
Wednesday

Holiday, Scotland and New Zealand

03
Thursday

04
Friday

05
Saturday

06
Sunday

● Epiphany

The North Downs, by Edward McKnight Kauffer, 1915

Two men and a rotary excavator at work deep underground, Topical Press, circa 1900

January

07
Monday

08
Tuesday

09
Wednesday

10
Thursday

11
Friday

12
Saturday

13
Sunday

January

14
Monday

15
Tuesday

16
Wednesday

17
Thursday

18
Friday

19
Saturday

20
Sunday

Sanders Phillips & Co. Ltd, The Baynard Press, London, S.W.9.

Hampton Court, by Charles Paine, 1921

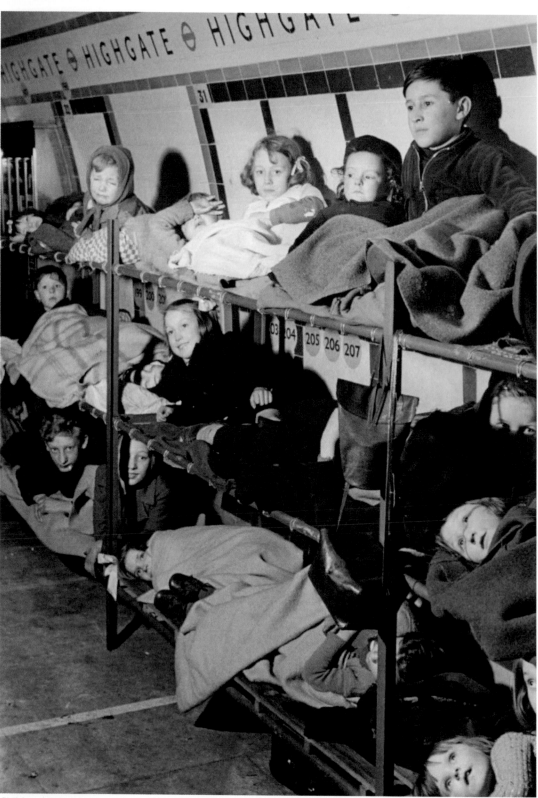

Children shelter in three-tier bunks at Highgate Underground station on the Northern line during the Second World War, Fox Photos, September 1940–March 1945

January

○ Holiday, USA (Martin Luther King Jnr Day)

21
Monday

22
Tuesday

23
Wednesday

24
Thursday

25
Friday

Australia Day

26
Saturday

☾

27
Sunday

January & February

Did you know?
The average
Tube train travels
184,269km a year

Holiday, Australia (Australia Day)

28
Monday

29
Tuesday

30
Wednesday

31
Thursday

01
Friday

02
Saturday

03
Sunday

HORACE
TAYLOR

BRIGHTEST LONDON
AND HOME BY

No. 1560 - 1000 - 19/11/24

THE DANGERFIELD PRINTING C? L?? LONDON

Brightest London and home by Underground, by Horace Taylor, 1924

Peaked cap, as issued to underground supervisory grade staff, 1995–2000

February

●

04
Monday

Chinese New Year

05
Tuesday

Accession of Queen Elizabeth II. Holiday, New Zealand (Waitangi Day)

06
Wednesday

07
Thursday

08
Friday

09
Saturday

10
Sunday

February

11
Monday

12
Tuesday

☽

13
Wednesday

14
Thursday

Valentine's Day

15
Friday

16
Saturday

17
Sunday

Southend-on-sea, by Verney L. Danvers, 1924

A member of staff poses beside a bell shelter, Topical Press, 1939

February

Holiday, USA (Presidents' Day)

18
Monday

○

19
Tuesday

20
Wednesday

21
Thursday

22
Friday

23
Saturday

24
Sunday

February & March

25
Monday

26
Tuesday

☽

27
Wednesday

28
Thursday

St David's Day

01
Friday

02
Saturday

03
Sunday

KENWOOD

LONDON'S NEW PARK

Nearest Station  HAMPSTEAD

Kenwood; Londons new park, by Walter E. Spradbery, 1925

Strand Underground station entrance, July 1907–December 1907

March

04
Monday

Shrove Tuesday

05
Tuesday

● Ash Wednesday

06
Wednesday

07
Thursday

08
Friday

09
Saturday

10
Sunday

March

11
Monday

Commonwealth Day

12
Tuesday

13
Wednesday

14
Thursday

☽

15
Friday

16
Saturday

17
Sunday

St Patrick's Day

Season tickets save trouble, by Clive Gardiner, 1928

View looking up escalators 1 and 2 at Earl's Court Underground station by H. K. Nolan, 28 February 1967

Holiday, Republic of Ireland and Northern Ireland (St Patrick's Day)

18
Monday

19
Tuesday

Vernal Equinox (Spring begins)

20
Wednesday

○

21
Thursday

22
Friday

23
Saturday

24
Sunday

March

25
Monday

26
Tuesday

27
Wednesday

☾

28
Thursday

29
Friday

30
Saturday

Mothering Sunday, UK and Republic of Ireland. British Summer Time begins

31
Sunday

UNDERGR

MANNER

NO WET · NO COLD

30/1000/4129

No wet – no cold, by Frederick Schneider Manner, 1929

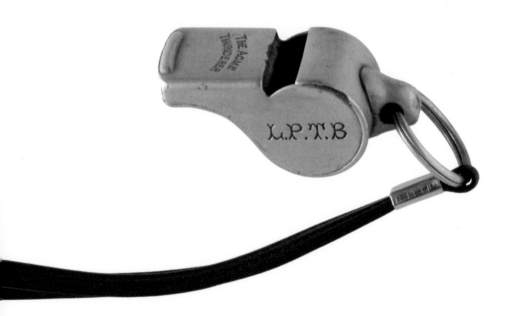

Whistle; as issued by LPTB staff, 1933–1947

April

01
Monday

02
Tuesday

03
Wednesday

04
Thursday

05
Friday

06
Saturday

07
Sunday

April

08
Monday

09
Tuesday

10
Wednesday

11
Thursday

12
Friday

☽

13
Saturday

Palm Sunday

14
Sunday

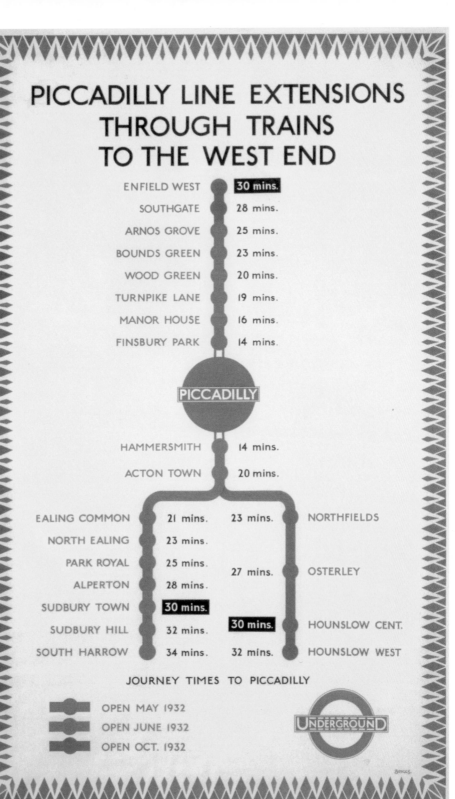

Timetable of Piccadilly line extensions, by Briggs, 1932

Easter 1930 by London's Underground, 1930

April

Week 16

15 Monday

16 Tuesday

17 Wednesday

Maundy Thursday

18 Thursday

○ Good Friday. Holiday, UK, Canada, Australia and New Zealand

19 Friday

First Day of Passover (Pesach)

20 Saturday

Easter Sunday. Birthday of Queen Elizabeth II

21 Sunday

April

Week 17

22
Monday

Easter Monday. Holiday, UK (exc. Scotland), Republic of Ireland, Australia and New Zealand

23
Tuesday

St George's Day

24
Wednesday

25
Thursday

Holiday, Australia and New Zealand (Anzac Day)

26
Friday

☾

27
Saturday

28
Sunday

PLEASE STAND ON THE RIGHT
OF THE ESCALATOR

Please stand on the right of the escalator, by Fougasse (Cyril Kenneth Bird), 1944

Framed glass 'tickets' sign with a flighted roundel arrow, from a passimeter at Essex Road station, circa 1936

April & May

29
Monday

30
Tuesday

01
Wednesday

02
Thursday

03
Friday

04
Saturday

05
Sunday

May

06

Monday

Early Spring Bank Holiday, UK. Holiday, Republic of Ireland.

First Day of Ramadân (subject to sighting of the moon)

07

Tuesday

08

Wednesday

09

Thursday

10

Friday

11

Saturday

12

Sunday

☽ Mother's Day, USA, Canada, Australia and New Zealand

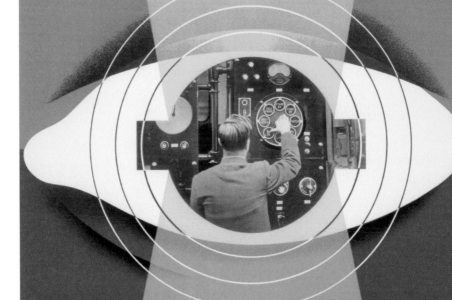

Behind the seen; at London's service, by James Fitton, 1948

Interior view of P-stock 'A' trailer car no. 13261, by Dr Heinz Zinram, 1963

Did you know?
Only 45% of the Tube network is underground

13
Monday

14
Tuesday

15
Wednesday

16
Thursday

17
Friday

18
Saturday

19
Sunday

May

Week 21

20

Monday

Holiday, Canada (Victoria Day)

21

Tuesday

22

Wednesday

23

Thursday

24

Friday

25

Saturday

☾

26

Sunday

Have you left anything behind?, by P. Gates, 1953

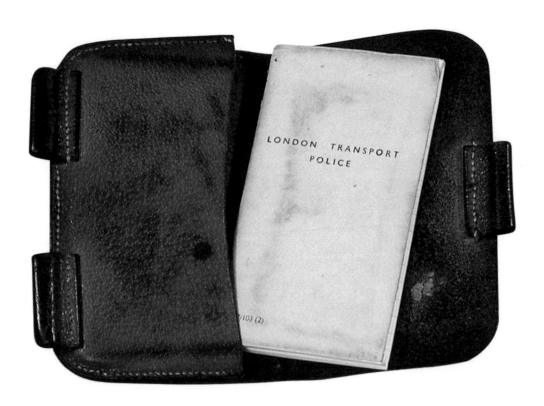

Wallet; for notebook, as issued to London Transport Police, 1934–1958

Spring Bank Holiday, UK. Holiday, USA (Memorial Day)

27
Monday

28
Tuesday

29
Wednesday

Ascension Day

30
Thursday

31
Friday

01
Saturday

Coronation Day

02
Sunday

June

Week 23

03

Monday

● Holiday, Republic of Ireland. Holiday, New Zealand (The Queen's Birthday)

04

Tuesday

05

Wednesday

Eid al-Fitr (end of Ramadân, subject to sighting of the moon)

06

Thursday

07

Friday

08

Saturday

The Queen's Official Birthday (subject to confirmation)

09

Sunday

Whit Sunday. Feast of Weeks (Shavuot)

See London by London Transport, by Harry Stevens, 1970

Baker Street affair, by Wozzy Dias, 1987

June

☽ Holiday, Australia (The Queen's Birthday)

10
Monday

11
Tuesday

12
Wednesday

13
Thursday

14
Friday

15
Saturday

Trinity Sunday. Father's Day, UK, Republic of Ireland, USA and Canada

16
Sunday

June

Did you know?
The Tube network measures 402km in total

17
Monday

○

18
Tuesday

19
Wednesday

20
Thursday

Corpus Christi

21
Friday

Summer Solstice (Summer begins)

22
Saturday

23
Sunday

LONDON HISTORY AT THE
LONDON MUSEUM
DOVER STREET
OR ST. JAMES'S PARK STATION

London history at the London Museum, by Edward McKnight Kauffer, 1922

London Passenger Transport Board (LPTB) shrapnel helmet, as issued to Road Spotters, 1939–1945

June

Week 26

24
Monday

☾

25
Tuesday

26
Wednesday

27
Thursday

28
Friday

29
Saturday

30
Sunday

July

01
Monday

Holiday, Canada (Canada Day)

02
Tuesday

●

03
Wednesday

04
Thursday

Holiday, USA (Independence day)

05
Friday

06
Saturday

07
Sunday

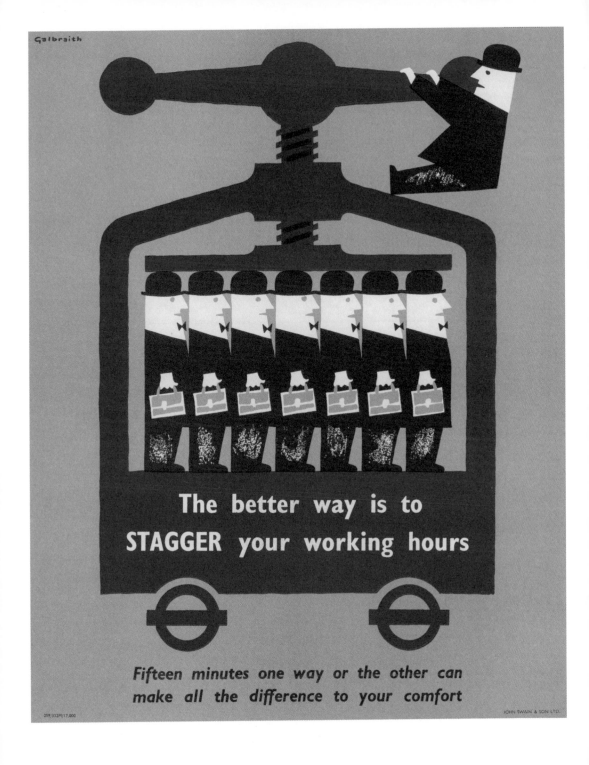

Stagger your working hours, by Victor Galbraith, 1959

Moquette used on Metrobus, Titan type buses, D78-stock and 1983-tube stock, circa 1975

July

Week 28

Did you know?
The shortest distance between stations is 0.3 km, Leicester Square to Covent Garden on the Piccadilly Line

08
Monday

☽

09
Tuesday

10
Wednesday

11
Thursday

Holiday, Northern Ireland (Battle of the Boyne)

12
Friday

13
Saturday

14
Sunday

July

15

Monday

St Swithin's Day

16

Tuesday

○

17

Wednesday

18

Thursday

19

Friday

20

Saturday

21

Sunday

ABCDEFGHIJKLMN
OPQRSTUVWXYZ
abcdefghijklmn
opqrstuvwxyz
1234567890
&£,.;:'""?!--*//()

ABCDEFGHIJKLMN
OPQRSTUVWXYZ
1234567890
&£,.;:'""?!--*()

Proof sheet showing Johnston Sans typeface, 1992

Night maintenance, 'fluffer' or underground tunnel cleaner at work, Topical Press, 1952

July

22
Monday

23
Tuesday

24
Wednesday

☾

25
Thursday

26
Friday

27
Saturday

28
Sunday

July & August

Week 31

29 Monday

30 Tuesday

31 Wednesday

01 Thursday

●

02 Friday

03 Saturday

04 Sunday

Trafalgar Square (now Charing Cross) Underground station, 1906–1908

UNDERGROUND

FOR HOME.

CRTM 1999/2343

SEASON TICKET RATES.

		3rd Class. 3 months.
		£ s. d.
EALING and		
Victoria	.. ..	1 10 0
Charing Cross	.. ..	1 18 6
Mansion House	.. ..	2 0 0
Knightsbridge	.. ..	1 10 0
Leicester Square	.. ..	1 18 6
King's Cross	.. ..	2 0 0
ACTON TOWN OR CHISWICK PARK and		
Earl's Court	.. ..	1 2 6
Victoria	.. ..	1 8 0
Charing Cross	.. ..	1 15 6
Hyde Park Corner	..	1 8 0
Temple	.. ..	1 15 6
Holborn	.. ..	1 15 6
HAMMERSMITH and		
Victoria	.. .. ..	1 2 6
Westminster	.. ..	1 7 0
Charing Cross	.. ..	1 7 6
Mansion House	.. ..	1 8 9
Knightsbridge	.. ..	1 2 6
Leicester Square	.. ..	1 7 6
TURNHAM GREEN and		
West Kensington	.. ..	1 1 0
Charing Cross	.. ..	1 12 6
Mansion House	.. ..	1 17 0
Knightsbridge	.. ..	1 8 0
Leicester Square	.. ..	1 12 6
Aldgate, East	.. ..	2 0 0

TRAIN SERVICES.

Hammersmith: 19 trains hourly in busy hours; 12 during the day.

Other Stations: Every 5 minutes in busy hours; every 6 minutes during the day.

25,000—100—7—8—12

Bookmark; published by the Underground Group, with hare in a field on obverse and underground season ticket rates on reverse, August 1912

August

Holiday, Scotland and Republic of Ireland

05
Monday

06
Tuesday

☽

07
Wednesday

08
Thursday

09
Friday

10
Saturday

11
Sunday

August

Week 33

12
Monday

13
Tuesday

14
Wednesday

○

15
Thursday

16
Friday

17
Saturday

18
Sunday

A member of London Transport staff affixes a poster outside an Underground station, Fox Photos, 1942

Keep Britain tidy (poster detail), 1958

August

Did you know?
The longest continuous tunnel is 27.8 km, from East Finchley to Morden on the Northern Line

19
Monday

20
Tuesday

21
Wednesday

22
Thursday

☾

23
Friday

24
Saturday

25
Sunday

August & September

26
Monday

Summer Bank Holiday, UK (exc. Scotland)

27
Tuesday

28
Wednesday

29
Thursday

●

30
Friday

31
Saturday

01
Sunday

Islamic New Year. Father's Day. Australia and New Zealand

Interior view of P-stock 'A' trailer car no. 13261, by Dr Heinz Zinram, 1963

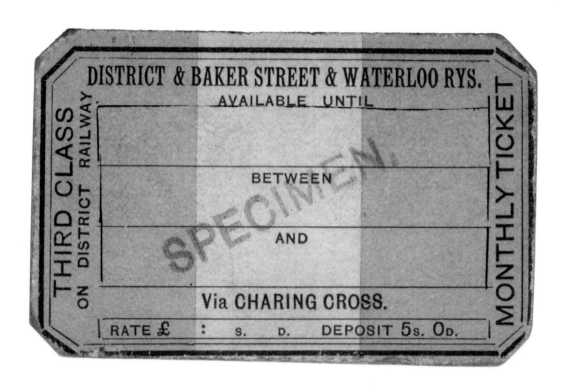

DISTRICT & BAKER STREET & WATERLOO RYS.

AVAILABLE UNTIL

THIRD CLASS
ON DISTRICT RAILWAY

BETWEEN

AND

Via CHARING CROSS.

RATE £   :   s.   d.   DEPOSIT 5s. 0d.

MONTHLY TICKET

SPECIMEN.

Specimen third class, monthly season ticket/pass, issued by District & Baker Street & Waterloo Railways, 1906–1910

September

Holiday, USA (Labor Day). Holiday, Canada (Labour Day)

02
Monday

03
Tuesday

04
Wednesday

05
Thursday

☽

06
Friday

07
Saturday

08
Sunday

September

09

Monday

10

Tuesday

11

Wednesday

12

Thursday

13

Friday

○

14

Saturday

15

Sunday

Sherlock Holmes motifs on Baker Street Underground station, Bakerloo line platform by Chorley Hyman & Rose, 1985

DLR train captain standing in the doorway of a train with her hand on the door controls, by Ian Bell, 1993

September

16
Monday

17
Tuesday

18
Wednesday

19
Thursday

20
Friday

21
Saturday

☾

22
Sunday

September

23
Monday

Autumnal Equinox (Autumn begins)

24
Tuesday

25
Wednesday

26
Thursday

27
Friday

28
Saturday

●

29
Sunday

Michaelmas Day

1:100 scale model of Balham station in 1926, 2007

Please avoid the rush hours, by Victor Galbraith, 1959

September & October

Jewish New Year (Rosh Hashanah)

30
Monday

01
Tuesday

02
Wednesday

03
Thursday

04
Friday

☽

05
Saturday

06
Sunday

October

07
Monday

08
Tuesday

09
Wednesday

Day of Atonement (Yom Kippur)

10
Thursday

11
Friday

12
Saturday

○

13
Sunday

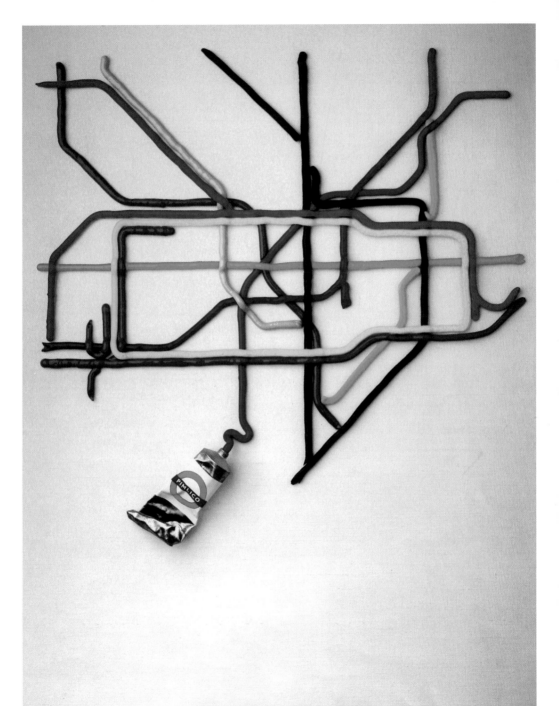

THE TATE GALLERY
by Tube

One of a series of new paintings commissioned by London Underground

The Tate Gallery by Tube, by David Booth of the agency Fine White Line, 1987

On sale here; season ticket cases, 1936

October

First day of Tabernacles (Succoth). Holiday, USA (Columbus Day). Holiday, Canada (Thanksgiving)

14
Monday

15
Tuesday

16
Wednesday

17
Thursday

18
Friday

19
Saturday

20
Sunday

October

21
Monday

☾

22
Tuesday

23
Wednesday

24
Thursday

25
Friday

26
Saturday

27
Sunday

British Summer Time ends

Eduardo Paolozzi tiling at Tottenham Court Road Underground station, 1982–1984

To town tonight, by Victor Galbraith, 1958

October & November

● Holiday, Republic of Ireland. Holiday, New Zealand (Labour Day)

28
Monday

29
Tuesday

30
Wednesday

Halloween

31
Thursday

All Saints' Day

01
Friday

02
Saturday

03
Sunday

November

Week 45

Did you know?
The busiest Tube station is Waterloo, with 100.3 million passengers per year

☽

04

Monday

Guy Fawkes

05

Tuesday

06

Wednesday

07

Thursday

08

Friday

09

Saturday

Remembrance Sunday

10

Sunday

A secure and interesting job, by Victor Galbraith, 1957

Night maintenance, staircase, Piccadilly Circus Underground station, Topical Press, 1952

November

Holiday, USA (Veterans Day). Holiday, Canada (Remembrance Day)

11
Monday

○

12
Tuesday

13
Wednesday

14
Thursday

15
Friday

16
Saturday

17
Sunday

November

18
Monday

19
Tuesday

☾

20
Wednesday

21
Thursday

22
Friday

23
Saturday

24
Sunday

Epsom summer meeting, by Andrew Power, 1933

A change of residence is as good as a holiday, by Charles Paine, 1929

November & December

25
Monday

●

26
Tuesday

27
Wednesday

Holiday, USA (Thanksgiving)

28
Thursday

29
Friday

St Andrew's Day

30
Saturday

First Sunday in Advent

01
Sunday

December

Did you know?
74% of waste from stations, depots and offices is recycled

02

Monday

03

Tuesday

04

Wednesday

05

Thursday

06

Friday

07

Saturday

08

Sunday

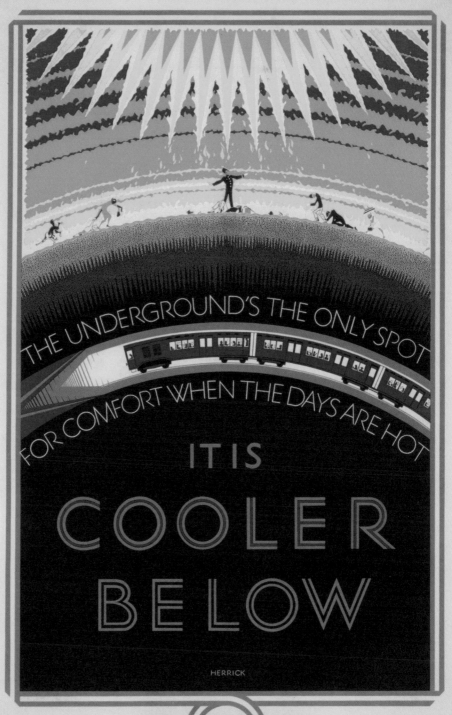

It is cooler below, by Frederick Charles Herrick, 1926

LDLTM
2000/19062

Architectural model of a section of the Jubilee Line Extension platform at Waterloo, circa 1995

December

09
Monday

10
Tuesday

11
Wednesday

12
Thursday

13
Friday

14
Saturday

15
Sunday

December

16
Monday

17
Tuesday

18
Wednesday

19
Thursday

☾

20
Friday

21
Saturday

22
Sunday

Winter Solstice (Winter begins). Hannukah begins (at sunset)

Hits the mark, scores always, by H. Roy Hazard, 1913

YOUR
CHRISTMAS
❖
ALL BRITISH
WHATEVER YOUR PLEASURE

Your Christmas, by Fougasse (Cyril Kenneth Bird), 1931

December

23
Monday

Christmas Eve

24
Tuesday

Christmas Day. Holiday, UK, Republic of Ireland, USA, Canada, Australia and New Zealand

25
Wednesday

● Boxing Day (St Stephen's Day).

Holiday, UK, Republic of Ireland, USA, Canada, Australia and New Zealand

26
Thursday

27
Friday

28
Saturday

29
Sunday

December & January

30
Monday

Hannukah ends

31
Tuesday

New Year's Eve

01
Wednesday

New Year's Day. Holiday, UK, Republic of Ireland, Canada, Australia and New Zealand

---

02
Thursday

Holiday, Scotland and New Zealand

03
Friday

04
Saturday

05
Sunday

Please shop between 10 and 4, by Victor Galbraith, 1959

Notes